Acting Out the Messages of Mark and John

Lenten Dialogues for Lectionary Cycle B

Roger E. Timm

CSS Publishing Company
Lima, Ohio

ACTING OUT THE MESSAGES OF MARK AND JOHN
LENTEN DIALOGUES FOR LECTIONARY YEAR B

FIRST EDITION
Copyright © 2014
by CSS Publishing Co., Inc.

For more information about CSS Publishing Company resources, visit our website at www.csspub.com, email us at csr@csspub.com, or call (800) 241-4056.

e-book:
ISBN-13: 978-0-7880-2802-1
ISBN-10: 0-7880-2802-2

ISBN-13: 978-0-7880-2801-4
ISBN-10: 0-7880-2801-4

PRINTED IN USA

Reviews for
Acting Out the Messages of Mark and John

At our mid-week Evening Prayer Services during Lent last year, our congregation used Pastor Timm's dialogues from his first book Acting Out Matthew's Messages. These lively, inspiring presentations were met with a great deal of affirmation and enthusiasm by members of the congregation. We anxiously await next Lent when we can use the dialogues in this publication as a part of our worship experience. In this book Pastor Timm has found fresh ways of presenting old texts from the gospels of Mark and John. Through some humorous and yet profound approaches, he offers fresh insights into familiar stories from scripture. I am sure these new approaches will awaken the power of these texts to affect people deeply. Although these dialogues are written to be presented as a part of corporate worship, I find that they lend themselves to personal reading and reflection as well. God speaks to us anew every day and every time we gather for worship. May these creative dialogues be among the ways God finds to speak to you and your congregation.

Rev. Lyn Langkamer, Interim Pastor
St. John's Lutheran Church, Emmaus, Pennsylvania

Pastor Timm's creative and original Lenten dialogues were so relevant and powerful when we first heard them that we encouraged him to publish them, and we are delighted that he did. The dialogues are extremely easy to use. At our soup suppers Pastor Timm would ask two people to be the characters, give them the scripts, practice once in the sanctuary (to be sure the microphones and inflections were good) and we were ready to go. All of the lessons were always well received by the congregation. Besides being user friendly, the dialogues are extremely meaningful. Each lesson had a contemporary feel: we felt that we were actually eye-witnesses to the events in Jesus' life. After each dialogue, there was always a powerful period of reflection as to what the dialogue means today for us as followers of Christ. Having been a member of Bible studies for decades, Pastor Timm's dialogues gave me a greater insight to the lessons than any other study guides. Your congregation will find that using this material will deepen their understanding and life in the gospel.

Diane Balin, Ph.D., and Jerry Balin
Members of Ascension Lutheran Church, Riverside, Illinois

How do we keep Lenten midweek worship alive? Pastor Roger Timm was unwilling to succumb to the growing trend of doing away with midweek Lenten worship. Instead, he developed series of short dialogues based on the Mark and John gospels for mid-week worship. As one who participated in the dialogues and also was a part of the worshiping congregation, I can say that mid-week Lenten worship took on a new meditative meaning. Each of the dialogues took on contemporary meaning as Pastor Timm ably took ancient words and made them feel as if they were be-ing spoken today. Any pastor who is looking for something new and meaningful to be used during midweek Lenten worship should give these dialogues a try. As a former bishop I know the struggles that pastors go through trying to keep midweek Lenten worship alive. Acting Out the Messages of Mark and John *will provide an excellent Lenten resource.*

Pastor Paul Landahl
Former Pastor of Ascension Lutheran Church, Riverside, Illinois
Former Bishop of the Metropolitan Chicago Synod, Evangelical Lutheran Church in America

With thanks to the people of St. James Lutheran Church of Naperville, Illinois — now Faith Lutheran Church of Aurora, Illinois — for inspiring the first of my dialogue series and setting me on the path to writing my subsequent dialogues, and with gratitude to my daughters, Sarah and Anne, for their support and encouragement.

Table of Contents

Affirming Our Baptismal Promises

Introduction

This book includes three series of Lenten dialogues based on the gospels of Mark and John, intended for use during Cycle B of the Revised Common Lectionary. (Mark is the primary gospel during Cycle B, but many readings from John are used during this cycle, especially in Lent.) Working with the assumption that Lent is a time for study and reflection and avoiding a focus on the Passion narrative before Holy Week, I wrote each of these series to explore messages from Mark and John from a slightly different perspective.

The first series, *The Secret Journal of St. James the Less,* was first presented when I was pastor of St. James Lutheran Church in Naperville, Illinois. When I was asked once which "James" we were named after, I learned that the congregation had been named after St. James the Less, son of Alphaeus, one of the twelve disciples. His mother, Mary, is also named in the gospel of Mark as one of the women who witnessed the crucifixion and came to the tomb on Easter morning. She may be included among the women referred to as accompanying Jesus during his ministry. With that background I imagined the "discovery" of the "journal" of St. James the Less and wrote these dialogues for our Lenten worship during a year of Cycle B, featuring conversations between James and his parents, Alphaeus and Mary. The dialogues focus on five key passages from the gospel of Mark. There are two differences from my other dialogue series: First, the second "dialogue" is actually a "trialogue," written as a conversation among James and both of his parents. Second, this series includes a "bonus" dialogue that presents Mark's Easter narrative, which was used at our Easter sunrise service.

The second series, *Generation One: The Impact of the Gospel on the First Generation of Believers — and Us,* includes conversations between first generation followers of Jesus. Specifically the first four dialogues are conversations between the apostle Peter and his wife, Anna. (Did Peter have a wife? Yes, Jesus did heal Peter's mother-in-law, and Paul talks about Peter, or Cephas, traveling with his wife in 1 Corinthians 9:5.) The last dialogue, which occurs after Peter's martyrdom, is a conversation between Anna and Junia, a leader in the Christian community in Rome and identified by Paul apparently as an apostle in Romans 16:7.

Because of the significant role that John plays in Cycle B, the third series, *Johannine Interviews*, consists of interviews with five people who are central to the narratives in the gospel of John. (One might argue that the adulterous woman is not really a Johannine character, but that narrative is quite important for our understanding of Jesus and we do have it now in our canonical version of John, even if it was inserted at some later point.) I wrote this series as if these people from John's gospel were being interviewed by radio or TV reporters. The reporters' names are not essential to the dialogues, but I thought that the surname "Evans" was appropriate for someone dealing with the "gospel"/"*euangelion*." "Angela" suggests an "angel," and angels are "messengers." I used "Harold" as a play on "herald angel." The call letters "WALC" refer to my congregation, Ascension Lutheran Church; those who use this set of dialogues should feel free to rename the station Angela and Harold work for.

This book also contains a "bonus" series of Lenten dialogues, based on the question posed to people affirming their baptismal promises in the Lutheran tradition:

> "You have made public profession of your faith. Do you intend to continue in the covenant God made with you in holy baptism:
> to live among God's faithful people,
> to hear the word of God and share in the Lord's supper,

to proclaim the good news of God
in Christ through word and deed,
to serve all people, following the example of Jesus,
and to strive for justice and peace in all the earth?"

I wrote this series because of the tradition that Lent is a time of preparation for baptism at the Easter celebration. The words of the affirmation of baptism are taken from *Evangelical Lutheran Worship*, the hymnal of the Evangelical Lutheran Church in America (ELCA), but the promises expressed have similar counterparts in other Christian denominations as well. The names here are not necessary for the dialogue. I use "Angela," however, to reflect her role as "messenger" and "Nova" because he is "new" to the faith.

These dialogues were used originally within a service of Evening Prayer that was part of a midweek Lenten gathering for a meal and worship. The dialogues could also be used in a Sunday worship service, a retreat setting, or an adult forum studying Mark or John.

We kept the setting for the dialogues simple — two chairs in front of the congregation, perhaps with a few props suggested by the specific skit. Such simple staging makes these dialogues usable in many contexts, but more elaborate use of props and stage settings may be helpful in reinforcing the message of each dialogue. The conversation in these dialogues is intended to be realistic and to express the good-natured banter that might occur between friends or family members. Dialogue participants should be encouraged to emphasize these moments of humor in the script.

The Secret Journal
of St. James the Less

Week 1

The Healing of the Paralyzed Friend

Mark 2:1-12

Narrator: We know him as "St. James the Less," for he was not as famous as that other James, the brother of John and the son of Zebedee, one of Jesus' inner core. But he was one of the twelve disciples of Jesus. James was the son of Alphaeus, and we hear him tonight talking with his mother, Mary.

James: Mother, you've got to come and listen to Jesus sometime.

Mary: Right, James, I can do all the cooking, all the sewing, and all the cleaning and still have hours to spare to come and listen to your crazy preacher friend. You can explain to your father, Alphaeus, why his supper isn't ready when he comes home from a hard day's work, fishing on the Sea of Galilee.

James: He's not crazy, Mom, and he's more than a friend. He's already asked Peter and the sons of Zebedee, James and John, to be his disciples, and I think he's going to ask me and my friend Thaddeus to follow him too.

Mary: What makes you think he's not crazy? His family is very embarrassed by him. They think he's crazy, and they're trying to figure out how to keep him at home. You don't think it's crazy to leave

James: a perfectly good job as a carpenter, where you're doing people some earthly good, and to begin wandering around the countryside pretending to heal people?

James: He's not *pretending* to heal people!

Mary: Really? When have you actually seen him heal anyone?

James: Today!

Mary: Today? What did you see? Are you sure you didn't imagine it?

James: Yes, I'm sure that I didn't imagine anything! Thaddeus and I were at the house where Jesus is staying in Capernaum. It was absolutely packed with people hanging on his every word. You have to come and hear him, Mom. He talks as if he knows exactly what God wants us to hear. Anyway, while we were listening to Jesus talk, we heard some people climbing up to the roof. I didn't think anything of it, for I know that Jesus himself likes to climb up there and pray. Suddenly there was a pounding noise and chunks of the roof started falling down. After a few minutes of this, there was a big hole in the roof and four people began to let this paralyzed man down in his cot right in front of Jesus.

Mary: What did he do?

James: That is what's strange. He didn't heal him right away. Instead he said, "Son, your sins are forgiven."

Mary: That's funny. Why didn't he heal him?

James: Wait, there's more. Besides, you know how people think that their sins cause their sickness.

Anyway, after he said that, some of the synagogue leaders were mumbling about it being blasphemous to forgive sins. "Only God can forgive sins," some were saying. Somehow Jesus knew what they were mumbling about. He said to them, "Which is easier, to tell this paralytic to get up and walk or to forgive his sins?" Then Jesus said, turning to the paralytic, "So you know that the Son of Man has the authority to forgive sins, I say to you: rise, pick up your mat, and go home." And he did!

Mary: That's really amazing, James. Are you sure you weren't seeing things?

James: I know it's amazing. Everyone there was totally surprised too. But I saw it with my own eyes. That's why you have to come and hear him.

Mary: All right, James, I'll talk with your father about this and find some way to come some time.

James: You know, Mom, what I find even more amazing about what Jesus does is that he doesn't seem to do it to show off. He tells people not to tell anyone about what he does, and he heals people because he feels compassion for them, not because he wants to be known for performing a miracle. And he hangs out with people no one else wants to be seen with — like tax collectors.

Mary: Really? Are you sure that's good, James? I don't like you hanging around with shady people.

James: Oh, Mom, don't worry! I don't think they're so shady.

Mary: You don't? I'm sure there are reasons why people don't want to be seen with these characters. Tax collectors especially. Everyone knows they work for those Romans and they overcharge us besides. You might get a bad reputation for whom you hang out with.

James: Don't judge people too quickly, Mom! Maybe you should come and meet some of these people. I don't know if I'll get a bad reputation or not but I've come to respect the people Jesus associates with. They're attracted to Jesus because they're sincerely seeking a relationship with God, and we're finding that with Jesus. You have to come and see for yourself!

Mary: All right, all right, but now it's time for supper!

Week 2

Teaching in Parables

Mark 4:1-20

Narrator: James convinced his mother, Mary, and father, Alphaeus, to join him in listening to Jesus preach. They're just returning home after hearing Jesus tell the crowds some parables along the shore of the Sea of Galilee.

Alphaeus: It sure was crowded down on the lakeshore. Everybody and his brother from the whole of Galilee must have been there.

James: Yes, but wasn't his sermon great?

Alphaeus: I guess, but I hope he's a better carpenter than he would be a farmer!

James: What do you mean by that?

Alphaeus: Any farmer worth his salt knows that you don't waste good seed by spreading it among the thorns, or on rocky ground, or on the hard, beaten-down soil of a path.

Mary: Oh, don't be so grumpy, Alphaeus! Don't you know that he was just telling a story to make a point? He wasn't really talking about farming.

Alphaeus: How come you're suddenly an expert on what this Jesus means? I thought James here was his follower.

Mary: Well, it just makes good sense. Jesus isn't wandering around the countryside to give lessons on farming. He's a prophet, preaching God's word.

James: So finally you see it, Mother! Jesus is a prophet!

Mary: Quiet, James, I'm arguing with your father.

Alphaeus: All right, so he's not talking about productive farming methods. Then what is his point?

Mary: James has been telling us about how some of the Pharisees follow Jesus around and try to find something wrong with what he does or says. Did you see those Pharisees hanging around the outskirts of the crowd?

Alphaeus: Actually, I did. So what?

Mary: Well, I think Jesus was talking about them and the others who don't want to accept what he has to say. I think Jesus was saying that he is like that sower and that he's going to have trouble getting a good response. Some people will accept his teaching, but others will oppose or resist it.

James: I don't know, Mother. I think Jesus meant more than that. Why do you think he made such a point of talking about all those different kinds of soil?

Mary: I thought those were just some details to make the story interesting.

James: Maybe, but I think he was talking about different kinds of people and the different ways they react to what Jesus has to say. I've seen this already. Some people don't listen to Jesus at all; it's like they close their ears and don't hear what he says. Some people listen and respond but after a while they don't come to hear Jesus anymore. And some listen and become his followers.

Alphaeus: How come you're so smart that you can figure out these funny stories of Jesus?

James: I guess I should be honest. I was talking with Thaddeus on the way home, and he was telling me that some of the other disciples asked Jesus what he meant, because they were confused by these stories Jesus was telling. Jesus was sad that they didn't catch on, and then he gave them this explanation of his story.

Mary: Why do you think Jesus tells these stories if no one can understand them? Doesn't he want people to know what he's saying? I mean, look at us — three of us and three different ideas about what he meant.

James: Thaddeus said one of the other disciples asked Jesus the same question, and he said that Jesus told them that he uses these stories he calls parables so that only those who genuinely want to follow him will understand. Just like you noticed today — some people listen to Jesus mostly to try to catch him saying something wrong.

Mary: So to understand these parables we need to have an open mind about Jesus and be willing to hear what he's telling us?

James: That's right.

Alphaeus: What about those different soils? Isn't Jesus being like a bad farmer and wasting his message on people who won't understand or who won't follow him like you do?

James: I think Jesus wants to give everyone a chance to hear his message and be faithful to God. That's a sign of his compassion for people. Maybe some people aren't ready to follow Jesus right now for some reason but at least they have heard Jesus invite them to be part of God's kingdom.

Mary: Well, I'm glad you insisted that we come and listen to Jesus. What's really important is not the exact meaning of what he said but how each of us responds to him. I do think God has sent him to us, and what he said made me feel like God was speaking to me, even if I didn't understand everything he meant. I want to go back and hear more.

Alphaeus: You can go back, Mary; I won't stop you. I'll get along fine when you're gone.

James: Dad, why don't you come and follow Jesus too? You ask some good questions that would help us all understand Jesus better.

Alphaeus: No, I don't think I'm the disciple type. You can be Jesus' disciple and tell me what he is teaching about God's will for us, but I think I can spend my time better in my boat catching some fish so that we can eat. We each have different ways to serve God. Besides, my friend Zebedee needs help now that his two sons are following this Jesus and have left him to tend the fishing nets alone.

The Feeding
of the Hungry Crowds

Mark 6:30-44

Narrator: Our disciple, James, son of Alphaeus and Mary, has just returned home after spending several days traveling around with Jesus and the other disciples.

Mary: What's wrong, James? You look like you've seen a ghost!

James: That's about how I feel.

Mary: Why? What happened?

James: I'm getting more confused about Jesus.

Mary: What has he done now? I thought you were convinced he is one of God's prophets. That's how I felt after I heard him tell us all those parables.

James: Well, I just had an unsettling couple of days. Remember how I told you that Jesus sent us twelve disciples out to preach and heal people? What an experience that was! How thrilling it was to see people listen to us like they do to Jesus and to see people be healed like Jesus does! We came back to Jesus and he could tell that we were all excited — but exhausted too. He told us to come with him to a deserted place to have some peace and quiet — to rest and to talk about our experiences.

Mary: I'm glad to hear that he has some sense. Since prophet-types don't always have a lot of common sense, I was afraid that neither he nor you and the rest of his disciples would get enough food or rest. But how could you get away to some quiet place with all those crowds following after you?

James: At first we climbed into the big fishing boat that belongs to Peter and started rowing across the Sea of Galilee, but even as fast as we were rowing we still couldn't get ahead of the crowds following us along the shore.

Mary: What did you do then?

James: Jesus obviously felt sorry for all the people following us. He said that they looked like lost sheep, wandering around aimlessly without their shepherd. So we went ashore and he taught them for most of the afternoon.

Mary: What did you do for dinner?

James: This is part of the reason I'm confused about Jesus. He's more than just a prophet.

Mary: Why do you say that?

James: Well, when we came to him and suggested that he dismiss the people so that they could go back home and eat something before it got too dark, he told us to give them something to eat.

Mary: How could you feed all those people? How many were there?

James: Five thousand men, not to mention all the women and children. We thought the same thing. We asked Jesus if he expected us to dig up some huge amount of money and go and buy enough to feed the huge crowd. Instead he asked us how much food we had. We checked around and found two fish and five loaves of bread.

Mary: Jesus thought that was enough food for such a huge crowd? Just like a man to be so unrealistic about food!

James: But he was right! We made the people sit down, and we distributed the food after Jesus had blessed it. The people had so much food left that we ended up with twelve baskets of leftovers.

Mary: You're kidding! How could he do that? No wonder you're confused about him. That is more than you'd expect from just a prophet.

James: Yes, but wait, it gets better — or more confusing. After feeding this crowd, Jesus told us to cross the lake while he found a secluded place to pray. After sunset a wind came up, and we were having a difficult time rowing and keeping the boat steady in the strong, gusty wind. You said that I looked like I had seen a ghost.

Mary: That's right, you look really pale.

James: Well, we thought we did see a ghost. While we were rowing in this storm, something or someone was walking on the water, going past our boat. It scared us to death!

Mary: Who, or what, was it?

James: It turned out to be Jesus. He got into the boat and the wind stopped.

Mary: How amazing!

James: Yes, it is, and that's why I'm confused. I don't know what to make of this Jesus. Is he a prophet, a teacher, a rabbi — or something more?

Mary: James, your story reminds me of when our people were wandering in the wilderness after they left Egypt; they were hungry too. Then God gave us this special food, manna, that kept us alive for forty years in the wilderness — that and the quails God sent us. Manna and quail wasn't much but it kept us alive. Bread and fish wasn't much, but it satisfied that crowd. Maybe God is doing something special through Jesus, just like God did when our people were freed from slavery in Egypt.

James: You're right, Mother. Jesus is like having God living among us again! But what do you think we should do about it?

Mary: I'm not sure that there's anything that we should do. God is the one doing something special. If we should do anything, we should open our eyes — or our hearts — to recognize what God is doing.

James: That's wise, Mother. I wonder if God is doing something similar for us like what God did back then, freeing our people from slavery in Egypt. What could Jesus be freeing us from?

Mary: That's something to think about. What is Jesus freeing us from now?

What the Rich Young Man Lacked

Mark 10:17-31

Narrator: Mary and Alphaeus, the parents of our disciple, James the Less, are talking over supper one evening just after James has returned to following Jesus after having spent a few days at home.

Alphaeus: Do you think it's healthy for us to let James follow after this Jesus person?

Mary: I don't know that there's anything we can do about it, Alphaeus. As young as James seems to us, he is a grown man and old enough to make his own decisions. Besides, Jesus inspires me too, and I would be following him all the time myself if I didn't have to keep up our household. Why do you ask if it's healthy for James to be following Jesus?

Alphaeus: I wonder because of something that James asked me while he was home. He asked me how much money we have around the house. I told him that we don't have much because most of the money I get for the fish I catch I use to buy food or to fix my nets.

Mary: I guess you didn't tell him about that jar you keep in the corner, stashed full of money.

Alphaeus: How do you know about that jar? I thought that was a secret hiding place!

Mary: Oh, I have my ways! You're not quite as clever as you think.

Alphaeus: All right, all right. But that is money I'm saving in case I can't go fishing, or I don't sell enough fish to buy our food, or maybe to pay for a trip to Jerusalem at Passover time some year. It doesn't really count as money that we have to use for our expenses.

Mary: Okay, but why did James want to know about our money?

Alphaeus: He wanted to know if he could have it to give to the poor people he meets as he travels around with Jesus.

Mary: Why would he want to do that?

Alphaeus: My question exactly! He said something about some person asking Jesus what he had to do to inherit eternal life. Jesus told him to keep the commandments. The young man said that he had kept all the commandments. Jesus told him then to sell all that he had and give it to the poor, and James said that he would like to do the same thing with the money we have. That sounds pretty strange to me and I wonder if Jesus is a healthy influence on James.

Mary: I don't know if James told you but I was with him when this young man came up to Jesus. You know, Jesus says things that aren't always easy to understand, and I wonder if James misunderstood what Jesus meant. This young man looked like he was very rich, and I wondered when Jesus said that he sensed that the young man was pretty attached to his wealth. Maybe Jesus sensed that this young man needed to let go of his possessions in order to be able to follow Jesus. Jesus went on to say, "It is easier for a camel to go through the eye of a needle than for a rich person to enter into the kingdom of God."

Alphaeus: That's ridiculous! No camel can get through that tiny hole in a needle.

Mary: That's right. "Who can be saved, then?" we asked. Jesus said, "With God, even things that seem impossible are possible." Good old Peter spoke up and said, "Well, Lord, we all have left our homes and families." Jesus assured him that all who left families and homes to follow him would be rewarded abundantly.

Alphaeus: Do you think Jesus wants James to give up all we own or not?

Mary: I think Jesus sensed that the young man was far too attached to what he owned. Maybe he kept the outward form of the commandments but his heart wasn't really dedicated to God. That's what Jesus wants — for us to be committed to God with all our heart, soul, and mind. James is like the other disciples who have already given up home and family to follow Jesus.

Alphaeus: Is my money jar safe for now, then?

Mary: I don't know, Alphaeus. Does it keep you from following Jesus?

Alphaeus: What keeps me from following Jesus is that I have to sit in my boat and catch some fish to feed you and James so that you can have enough energy to follow this Jesus around!

Mary: Don't be so grouchy, Alphaeus! Maybe Jesus would tell you to sell your boat, but maybe he would tell you to do your fishing in a spirit of gratitude to God and caring for people — James, me, and others too.

Alphaeus: Are you saying that loving God doesn't necessarily mean that we have to give up what we do in our regular lives?

Mary: Yes, that's right, but it does have something to do with our attitude. Are we trying to be faithful to God? Are we thankful for how God has blessed us? Do we look for ways to care for and help others?

Alphaeus: Those are heavy questions. So you don't think that Jesus is an unhealthy influence on James?

Mary: No, I think that James doesn't always understand exactly what Jesus means. But that's okay; I don't always get Jesus' point either. What I think is good for James — and for you and me — is that Jesus is trying to help him see that God wants us to give our whole heart and soul and mind to God.

Alphaeus: That's healthy?

Mary: Yes, but not easy.

Alphaeus: Okay, I'll stop worrying about James. Now I'll just have to worry about finding a new place to hide my money.

Week 5

The Misguided Disciples

Mark 10:32-45

Narrator: With the consent of her husband, Alphaeus, Mary, the mother of our disciple, James the Less, is now accompanying Jesus and his disciples as Jesus is making his way to Jerusalem. One evening James came to talk with his mother, visibly upset.

James: Those sons of Zebedee, I don't know who they think they are. They're only sons of a fisherman, just like me, but they act like they're special — like they're royalty or something. It's not enough that Jesus treats them special — along with Peter — but they want even more power.

Mary: What's gotten you so upset, James? Are you sure you aren't just jealous of them? I know you wish that you could be as close to Jesus as they and Peter are.

James: Maybe I am a little jealous. I do wish I could be as close to Jesus as they are, but I also see that they are good leaders who help Jesus a lot.

Mary: Then what's the problem? Did something happen today to upset you?

James: Yes. While we were walking today, James and John caught up to Jesus. While they were alone, they asked Jesus if they could sit at his right hand and at his left when he comes in glory.

Mary: What do you suppose that means?

James: It means they want to be his next-in-command when Jesus overthrows the Romans and ushers in his messianic kingdom. I suppose they want us other disciples to be their gofers or something while they lord it over the rest of us.

Mary: What did Jesus say?

James: Oh, he asked them if they could drink the cup he drinks or be baptized with the baptism he is baptized with. They said, "Yes," of course, and then he said that they would do that but the privilege of sitting on his right or left was something that only God could grant.

Mary: You know, James, I'm really surprised that Zebedee's sons asked Jesus that special favor.

James: Why does it surprise you? Don't you know how stuck on themselves they are?

Mary: That's not why I'm surprised. Didn't you hear today how Jesus told us — for the third time, I think — how he will be arrested and ridiculed and killed in Jerusalem? Then he said something strange about rising again after three days. But hearing that, James, made me feel really sad and depressed — and afraid. I don't know how James and John could be thinking about some glorious victory. Jesus surely wasn't talking about some victory over the Romans. Weren't they listening?

James: Maybe they were listening but not paying attention. Anyway the rest of us got really angry with them. Then Jesus took us aside and said that we should be different than other groups. Whoever wants to be our leader, he said, should act like our slave. Then he said something that really stuck with me, although I don't understand what he meant. He said, "For the Son of Man came, not to be served, but to serve and to give his life as a ransom for many."

Mary: You see, that's just what I mean!

James: What do you mean, that's what you mean?

Mary: Maybe you don't get it either! Zebedee's sons can dream all they want about being some important deputy general for the victorious conqueror of the Romans, but that's not what Jesus came for. Jesus is saying that he came, not to win some glorious victory, but to be like a slave or a servant.

James: You're right, but I don't know what to make of it. That's not the kind of messiah we are expecting.

Mary: You know, what Jesus told you reinforces what I've been thinking. I don't know what's going to happen in Jerusalem. I feel very apprehensive. But whatever it is, I think Jesus is doing something to serve us. Somehow what he'll do will be a sacrifice for us.

James: A servant who suffers for us. That's sure different from a conquering war hero. I think you're right about who Jesus thinks he is, Mom, but it won't be easy for me to get used to that idea.

Mary: I think he's trying to get us to see that God's way is a way, not of power and glory, but of love and compassion.

James: This adds something else that is difficult. Not only do we have to get used to Jesus being a servant who suffers, but also we need to have a different goal for ourselves. We disciples think that we might have a lot of power and influence in Jesus' kingdom, but if you're right our goal will be to serve others in that same loving way Jesus shows compassion to people in need. Any power-hungry disciple misses the point of what Jesus came for.

Mary: Yes, James, following Jesus will mean showing love and compassion, not having power and glory in Jesus' kingdom.

James: That'll be a surprise for those uppity sons of Zebedee!

Mary: Maybe for you too, James!

James: Okay, okay. I wonder if that's what Jesus meant by drinking the cup he will drink. I wonder if we'll have to drink that same cup. What will that mean for us who follow Jesus?

The Frightened Women

Mark 16:1-8

Narrator: Mary, the mother of our disciple, James the Less, has returned to the upstairs room in Jerusalem where James and the other disciples have been hiding since the arrest of Jesus.

James: Mother, what's wrong? Now you're the one who looks like you've seen a ghost!

Mary: I have — or at least I think I have. Actually I'm not sure what I've seen!

James: What in the world are you talking about? You're not making any sense!

Mary: James, I know that I may not be making any sense, but I just had a very upsetting and frightening experience.

James: What happened?

Mary: Well, you know that Mary Magdalene and Salome and I were watching Friday when Jesus was crucified. How awful that was! We saw when he died and we saw when Joseph of Arimathea came and took down his body from the cross. We followed at a distance because we wanted to see where Joseph was putting his body.

James: Why did you do that? Don't you know that could have been dangerous?

Mary: We didn't care if it was dangerous or not. We wanted to see where Joseph was taking Jesus' body so that we could come back and give him a proper burial. There wasn't enough time to do it on Friday before the sabbath began.

James: So that's why you got up so early this morning, to go to Joseph's tomb and complete Jesus' burial?

Mary: Yes. After we left, though, we realized that we hadn't thought carefully about what we would have to do. We had the burial spices but we didn't know how we would roll that huge stone away from the entrance into the tomb.

James: That's right! You should have asked me to come along!

Mary: Oh, James, all you disciples seemed too frightened and upset to bother to come along to help us.

James: From the way you look, maybe we were right!

Mary: When we arrived at the tomb, the stone had been rolled away. At first we were relieved, because all the way to the tomb we had been talking about how to roll that stone away. But then we began to feel frightened. Who had rolled the stone back? Were there some soldiers around? Had something eerie happened? And then we saw this bright light that blinded us. After my eyes adjusted a bit, I looked up and I saw a young man — I think — who told us that Jesus was raised and was not in the tomb. He told us to tell you to go to Galilee to meet Jesus.

James: Was that the ghost you saw?

Mary: Yes, but not exactly. I mean, he wasn't a ghost. He was very much alive and talked to us like a person, but he was so bright that he must have been an angel. I'm not sure what to think. The whole experience — finding the tomb empty, seeing this amazing person, and hearing what he said about Jesus — all this was very upsetting and frightening for us. We ran back here as fast as we could. What do you think this all means, James?

James: I don't know. Are you sure this person wasn't the caretaker for the tombs there — or someone playing a trick on you — or were you even seeing things? These past few days have been very stressful for all of us.

Mary: How crazy do you think your mother is, James? I know I've been stressed out like other followers of Jesus, but I know I wasn't imagining this person and he was no gardener either.

James: All right, mother; I don't think you're crazy. But if Jesus is alive, where is he? Why didn't he come here to see us? Could this be a trap planned by the people who hated him?

Mary: We won't know until we see him, but remember how Jesus said that he would have to die — and then rise again? When he said that, I was confused because I didn't know what he meant. Maybe this is what he meant.

James: Following Jesus surely has been one surprise after another! If God raised Jesus from the dead, what will this mean for us?

Mary: For one thing it shows that death no longer has the last word.

James: Right, and I think it's going to mean lots of new and different things for us. We thought we were disciples of God's special prophet, or maybe the Messiah who would free us from the Romans. Jesus is much more than that. I don't know whether to feel happy that Jesus is alive or frightened about what this will all mean for us.

Mary: I agree. My feelings are very mixed. Joy surely came this morning with the empty tomb, but it's frightening too. God has done something very different and awesome, and I don't know what it will mean for us. Our lives will be changed, I'm sure.

James: We don't know what this will mean for us yet, but I expect that we'll find out soon. I'd better tell Thaddeus and the other disciples. Where did this shining person say we should go?

Mary: Go back to Galilee. And, James, I believe you're right. From now on everything is going to be different.

James: You know, Mother, we of all people should know that God continually surprises us. This is one more and very special surprise!

Generation One:
The Impact
of the Gospel
on the First Generation
of Believers — and Us

Week 1

Do You Understand My Teaching in Parables?

Mark 4:1-20

Narrator: Peter and his wife, Anna, are staying with friends in Caesarea — more accurately, Caesarea Maritima — where they have just returned from visiting with Cornelius, the God-fearing Roman centurion who had a vision that he should send for Peter in nearby Joppa.[1] At that time Peter was still uncertain that he should associate with Gentiles, but in his own vision God told Peter not to call unclean what God had made clean. Peter went to Cornelius' house and ended up baptizing him and the believers with him. Anna and Peter recall that incident:

Anna: It was very heartening to see how faithful Cornelius is and how the gathering of believers in his home has grown.

Peter: Yes, it is — and how amazing it is that it all began with a message that I found so difficult to understand!

Anna: What message was that?

Peter: Do you remember how I told you about that vision I had in Joppa while I was on the roof waiting for lunch? I saw all these unclean, non-kosher animals being lowered in a sheet and a voice told me to kill and eat them. I said "No," because I'd never eaten anything unclean before.

The voice said, "Don't call unclean what I have made clean." After the vision was repeated three times, the messengers from Cornelius came.

Anna: Did you understand that God was telling you that it was all right for you to go and preach to Cornelius and the other Gentiles?

Peter: Not at first. It was so confusing to me. The vision told me to do something that seemed so wrong to me, and I didn't understand what the point was until later.

Anna: Wasn't Jesus' teaching like that too?

Peter: What do you mean?

Anna: I remember when you first started following Jesus that you would tell me some of his parables and how difficult you found them to understand.

Peter: Right. One of the earliest was his story about the farmer sowing seeds. At first I thought it seemed so simple. I could picture farmers around Capernaum out in their fields, sowing their seeds. Not all the seeds would fall on the best soil; some would go on the pathways or on rocky ground or among the thorns. It made me glad I was a fisherman instead of a farmer!

Anna: If this story was so much like our farmers' experience, why was it difficult for you to understand?

Peter: Jesus was often like this — he told a story that seemed very ordinary but it had a strange twist. At the end of this story he talked about how the good soil produced 30 times the seed sown in some places and then 60 and even 100 times in others. That never happens! Thirty times would be a miracle, let along 60 or 100. What was he trying to say?

Anna: What *was* he trying to say?

Peter: When we asked him, he said he taught in parables so that those outside our group would "see, but not perceive; would hear, but not understand." But Jesus said we were given the secret of God's kingdom.

Anna: If you were given the secret, how come you didn't understand?

Peter: Good question.

Anna: I think it means that some people just don't get the good news about Jesus, or they believe for a while and then fall away, but for those who do believe, God can bring amazing results.

Peter: That's what Jesus told us later when we asked him to explain the parable! How did you get that so easily?

Anna: Isn't it obvious?

Peter: Not to me, it wasn't!

Anna: What puzzles me more is why Jesus would say that he taught in parables so that people would *not* understand.

Peter: That puzzled me too. And it seemed that Jesus meant he purposely taught in parables so that people wouldn't understand, or it could be that his using parables was simply confusing to people, whether he intended that or not.

Anna: Either way, his parables weren't always clear to people who heard him. Why do you think Jesus taught that way?

Peter: I think one reason was that almost from the beginning there were some people who tried to trap him into saying something wrong. Using parables made that difficult.

Anna: So parables were a kind of self-defense.

Peter: Yes, but I also think that Jesus was looking for people who really wanted to understand him.

Anna: What do you mean?

Peter: Jesus was looking for people who would set aside expectations and be open to new ways of thinking about God. These parables that seemed like stories about ordinary life but had a surprising twist could open up new ways of understanding God and God's will for us.

Anna: So, if Jesus picked you as a disciple, how come you didn't listen that way?

Peter: Ask Jesus! Maybe he liked the challenge of working with thick-headed people like me.

Anna: As much as I love you as my husband, Peter, you surely can be thick-headed.

Peter: Thank you for being so affirming!

Anna: Well, you did get it eventually.

Peter: Yes, and I think we need to keep asking ourselves if we're open to hearing what Jesus is teaching us.

Anna: So listening to a parable means setting aside what we expect to hear and preparing ourselves to hear something new or challenging.

Peter: Yes, Jesus may lead us in ways that change us.

Anna: *(turning to the congregation)* Do you understand what Jesus is teaching *you*?

---

1. For a reference to Peter traveling with his wife, see 1 Corinthians 9:5.

Week 2

What Does Jesus' Healing Touch Mean for You?

Mark 5:21-43

Narrator: Peter and his wife, Anna, have moved on from Caesarea Maritima and now are staying with his friend Simon the tanner in Joppa. As they visit with their friends in Joppa, they are reminded about the time Peter came to Joppa and brought Dorcas back to life. Dorcas was very important in the community of disciples there for helping widows and others in need.

Anna: The disciples here in Joppa seem so grateful to you, Peter, for how you helped them by bringing Dorcas back to life for them.

Peter: That was quite a day for me. I was staying nearby in Lydda when two men from here came and begged me to come back with them to Joppa. They didn't tell me exactly what was wrong but they said that an important disciple from their group was gravely ill.

Anna: They didn't tell you that Dorcas had died?

Peter: No, they just wanted me to hurry up here.

Anna: You weren't prepared for what you saw here?

Peter: No, not really. They ushered me into the room where they had prepared her for burial. She had been very helpful to the widows in their community. A number of them were there weeping and they showed me some of the things she had given them. They were at a loss to know what to do after she was gone. I wasn't all that sure about what to do but I asked them to go outside the room. I knelt down and prayed beside her. The Spirit moved me to say to her, "Tabitha, get up!"

Anna: Tabitha? I thought her name was Dorcas.

Peter: Dorcas, Tabitha; they used both names. They both mean "gazelle." Apparently her generosity was both quick and graceful!

Anna: What happened then?

Peter: After I said that to her, she got up. I brought her out to the disciples and, of course, they were all filled with great joy.

Anna: I'm sure they were. You helped heal a great void in their community.

Peter: Yes, I did, but it wasn't really me. It was the Spirit of Christ working through me. That day reminds me of one amazing day with Jesus. In fact, saying "Tabitha, get up" reminds me of what Jesus said that day, "Talitha, get up."

Anna: Isn't that the day when Jesus healed a woman who had been bleeding for twelve years and then raised the daughter of Jairus, the leader of a synagogue?

Peter: Yes, that's the day, and it was only James and John and I who were with Jesus when he told the little girl to get up and brought her back to life.

Anna: Was that the first time Jesus singled the three of you out as leaders among his disciples?

Peter: Pretty much it was, yes. I'm sure you'll remind me not to get a big head about it!

Anna: You're right!

Peter: I know that during my time with Jesus I had my ups and downs, but it was special to see first-hand his power to heal.

Anna: I'm sure it was. What has always impressed me about the healings that day was how Jesus was not hesitant to risk becoming impure by being touched by this woman who was bleeding or by touching the dead girl.

Peter: That was Jesus. His love for others outweighed boundaries we were used to.

Anna: Was it his love that prompted his healings? I thought it was his way to show that he was the one God sent for us.

Peter: That was part of it. He often quoted the prophets who talked about how God would send healing for the blind and the lame, but I saw again and again that he healed people because of his deep compassion for them.

Anna: It was because of their faith too.

Peter: Yes. He told that woman, "Your faith has made you well." Jesus could tell when people trusted him and believed he had God's healing power.

Anna: You know, I see a similarity between you bringing Dorcas back to life and what Jesus did for Jairus' daughter and that woman.

Peter: What's that, Anna?

Anna: Just as you restored Dorcas to the community of disciples who relied on her so much, what Jesus did restored the girl and the woman to their communities — the girl was given back to her family and the woman no longer suffered the impurity that kept her from being fully part of her community.

Peter: Well, when we talk about *shalom*, or peace, isn't that what we mean — being restored to wholeness ourselves as well as with the people around us?

Anna: I just thought of something. Didn't you tell me that while Jesus was in the crowd going to Jairus' house, that he asked who touched him?

Peter: Yes, we all thought he was crazy. We were jammed together in a crowd. How could he sense some particular touch? He said that he felt some of his power go out of him.

Anna: So is Jesus' power a power for healing?

Peter: Yes, I think it is. Jesus used his power for healing in many ways. I believe he still does. I believe that I could bring Dorcas back to life only because the Spirit of Christ was working through me. After Jesus was raised back to life, we began to realize how powerful the love of God is that we saw in Jesus.

Anna: Back on that special day, then, you began to see the power of God to bring healing.

Peter: Yes, especially the kind of healing that means being restored to a loving relationship with God and with God's people.

Anna: I see that God's power and love work together to deepen our trusting relationship with God.

Peter: Yes, and our loving relationships with each other too.

Anna: *(turning to the congregation)* What does God's healing touch in Christ mean for *you*?

Who Do You Say That I Am?

Mark 8:27-38

Narrator: The apostle Peter and his wife, Anna, are enjoying some "R&R" from their missionary travels at the Springs of Pan, a first-century equivalent of a resort, where Philip, one of the sons of Herod the Great, had built a city in honor of himself and the Roman emperor, naming it Caesarea Philippi — another Caesarea besides Caesarea Maritima. This is the place where Jesus asked his disciples, "Who do you say that I am?" Their conversation begins after they've shared a midday meal along the banks of the stream.

Peter: When Jesus called us to fish for people instead of fish, I thought that would be easier than the hard work I had to do to net fish on the Sea of Galilee, but I really needed this rest from our travels to share the good news about Jesus.

Anna: I needed a break too, but what about it seems so difficult to you?

Peter: Just the travel itself is exhausting, hiking back and forth between Jerusalem and Galilee and into Asia Minor.

Anna: And staying in people's homes isn't always easy or pleasant.

Peter:	Right, but figuring out how to preach about Jesus is difficult too. That apostle Paul always seems to find some new way to challenge what I say or do. He is so obsessed with reaching out to Gentiles that he continually makes us rethink how we follow Jesus, whether we're Jews or Gentiles. Relaxing by these springs is a welcome change.
Anna:	Isn't this where Jesus brought you and the other disciples once?
Peter:	Yes, it is. This is where he asked us who people were saying he was. Then he asked us, "Who do *you* say that I am?"
Anna:	Isn't that when you answered for the disciples?
Peter:	Yes, I replied, "You are the Messiah."
Anna:	My dear husband, I've always been proud of how bold you can be.
Peter:	Well, maybe you shouldn't be so proud of me.
Anna:	Why not?
Peter:	Back then I had a very different idea of what kind of messiah Jesus was. I expected him to lead us in overthrowing the Romans. Right after I said he was the Messiah, Jesus talked about how he had to suffer and die. That was no way to be a successful messiah, so I took him aside and tried to correct him. That's when in front of all the other disciples he said to me, "Get behind me, Satan!" I was very embarrassed and upset.
Anna:	You've never told me much about that part of the story.
Peter:	Well, it wasn't one of my proudest moments. Now, of course, it seems so clear. Jesus' suffering and death was a result of how he lived out

the fullness of God's love, and God's raising him from the dead showed us the new way of love and peace that comes from what Jesus did. It is a whole new way of being the Messiah and now I get to share that good news.

Anna: How would you answer Jesus' question now?

Peter: He is so much more than what I meant by messiah. He is the Son of God. He saves us from sin and death. He calls us into a new relationship with God based on our faith and trust in him. And there was something else he said back then that I didn't quite understand because I was so upset.

Anna: What's that?

Peter: Jesus said that whoever wants to follow him needs to deny themselves and take up their cross.

Anna: Are we all going to get crucified? I worry about that sometimes.

Peter: I don't know; that might happen. But I don't think that's what he meant. He meant that following him means a life of loving and serving others.

Anna: Then my mother got it right.

Peter: Do you have to bring up your mother?

Anna: I know that you have always been a little uncomfortable around my mother. But I think she was a good disciple.

Peter: What do you mean?

Anna: Remember when Jesus healed her of her fever?

Peter: Yes, I do. It was one of his very first healings.

Anna: And what did she do?

Peter: I remember that she got up and fed all of us.

Anna: That is right. That was so like my mother. She was always getting food ready to feed her family. I thought she should have rested more, but she said, "No."

Peter: Why did she insist on feeding us?

Anna: For one thing, she thought of preparing food as her place in our family, and for another, she had a sense that an appropriate response to Jesus' healing was to respond with loving service in return.

Peter: So she was a good disciple by serving us?

Anna: Yes, exactly.

Peter: So who would *she* say Jesus is?

Anna: Jesus is the one who came from God to love and heal me so that I can love and heal others.

Peter: Maybe I'll have to admit that sometimes your mother is right!

Anna: That's not a bad idea, Peter!

Peter: I don't want to admit that she's right all the time, but I agree that the important part of being a disciple of Jesus is to find ways to respond to his love by offering others loving service like his.

Anna: Then if we say that Jesus is our Messiah, we will want to find ways to love others like he did.

Peter: Exactly. Who we say Jesus is will show up in how we live.

Anna: *(turning to the congregation)* Who do *you* say Jesus is?

What Does the Glory of Christ Mean for You?

Mark 9:1-13

Narrator: The apostle Peter and his wife, Anna, are enjoying some "R&R" from their missionary travels at the Springs of Pan, a first-century equivalent of a resort, where Philip, one of the sons of Herod the Great, had built a city in honor of himself and the Roman emperor, naming it Caesarea Philippi. Peter and Anna are continuing their lunchtime conversation. They had just finished talking about Peter's response to Jesus' question, "Who do you say that I am?" Now Peter turns to a new topic, his experience of Jesus' transfiguration.

Peter: Since we've been talking about the high and low of my answer to Jesus' question, "Who do you say that I am," I should tell you something else.

Anna: What's that?

Peter: It's something I haven't told you before.

Anna: You mean there are things you haven't shared with me?

Peter: Not many, but this is one of them.

Anna: *One* of them? I'm curious about what these things are you haven't told me about.

Peter: What I want to tell you is the only important thing I haven't told you about.

Anna: Uh-huh. Go ahead and tell me. I'll worry about the other things some other time.

Peter: What I want to tell you about is a really strange experience James and John and I had about a week later.

Anna: Why didn't you tell me about this before?

Peter: Jesus said that we shouldn't tell anyone about it until after he rose from the dead. For one thing, at that point we didn't have a clue about what that meant. Then with all the turmoil after his crucifixion and the resurrection I forgot about this experience.

Anna: That's a reasonable excuse, I guess, but you can tell me now.

Peter: I think I've told you that Jesus would often go up on a mountain to pray. Sometimes he would go alone but this time he asked James, John, and me to go with him.

Anna: Did you pray with him?

Peter: No, we didn't have time.

Anna: You didn't? Why not?

Peter: No sooner had we gotten to the top of the mountain than suddenly Jesus was shining as bright as the sun. I've never seen anything so dazzling white.

Anna: How strange that must have seemed! Were you frightened?

Peter: Yes, but there's more! At the same time we saw Jesus talking with Moses and Elijah.

Anna: What? Were you having a hallucination?

Peter: No, it was definitely a real experience.

Anna: How did you know it was Moses and Elijah he was talking with? I don't think you've ever seen them.

Peter: No, I haven't met them! Somehow I just knew. Besides I heard Jesus calling them by name.

Anna: What were they talking about?

Peter: I didn't really hear any details. The experience was so overwhelming.[1]

Anna: What did you do then?

Peter: Remember how you said that you've always been proud of how bold I can be?

Anna: Yes, except when your boldness means you stick your foot in your mouth. What was it this time?

Peter: Another "foot-in-my-mouth" time.

Anna: What did you say this time?

Peter: I wasn't sure what to make of the presence of Moses and Elijah. It was scary but also exciting. I think of them as representing the law and the prophets, the two pillars of our faith. How special, I thought, to spend some time together with them and Jesus. So I said, "How good it is to be here, teacher. Let us make three booths — one for you, one for Moses, and one for Elijah." I was thinking of our Feast of Tabernacles when we remember our time of wandering in the wilderness.

Anna: What was wrong with that? That sounds like a good idea to me. What a privilege to be on the mountain with Jesus, Moses, and Elijah!

Peter: Thanks for sympathizing with me! But I'm sure now that it wasn't the right thing to say.

Anna: Why not?

Peter: Because suddenly we were covered in something like a cloud and a voice from heaven spoke, "This is my Son, the Beloved, listen to him!" When we looked up again, there was no one there but Jesus.

Anna: Hearing that voice must have been eerie, even frightening.

Peter: Yes, it was, but I understood the voice to mean that I was wrong to put Jesus in the same category as Moses and Elijah. I understand now that Jesus wasn't just another of the prophets, no matter how special they were. Jesus is the Son of God!

Anna: We know that now after he rose from the dead.

Peter: Yes, we do now, but we didn't know what he was talking about then.

Anna: I'm glad you shared this story with me, even if it was a time when you spoke too quickly without thinking. After all this time what do you think that your mountaintop experience of the glory of Jesus means?

Peter: For one thing, this experience was one more time that God was leading me to recognize who Jesus really was. He wasn't the kind of messiah I was expecting; he wasn't merely a teacher or even a prophet. No, he was — he is — the Son of God! It took the other disciples and me a lot of time to realize how special Jesus is. But that's not all.

Anna: What else? Recognizing this shining glory of Jesus as a sign of his being God's own Son seems like quite enough.

Peter: Remember how the voice from heaven said, "Listen to him!" If Jesus is the Son of God, then what he taught us is what God wants us to know and do. I see now that God wants us to follow the way of love that Jesus showed us. I'm still growing in what that means — a love that reaches out to people not loved by others, a love that means bearing burdens and even suffering.

Anna: I can see that you learned a lot from that mountaintop experience.

Peter: Yes, I can say that now.

Anna: *(turning to the congregation)* What does the glory of Christ mean for *you*?

---

1. Mark doesn't describe any details of Jesus' conversation with Moses and Elijah. Luke (9:31) says they were discussing Jesus' departure — *exodus* in Greek.

How Do You Respond to the Empty Tomb?

Mark 16:1-8

Narrator: Today's setting is somewhat somber. Anna, Peter's wife is now a widow. She is talking with Junia, a Christian in Rome, identified by the apostle Paul as a leader in that community and an apostle (Romans 16:7). They have just come from their regular Sunday evening gathering for worship and Eucharistic meal in one of the catacombs where Christians meet outside Rome. The time is a few years after the Emperor Nero burned Rome down and then blamed the Christians, persecuting and killing many of them, including both Peter and Paul. This evening they heard the reading of the story of Jesus' life written by Mark, who had been a close associate of Peter. The ending had seemed quite abrupt to them.

Junia: Was it difficult for you, Anna, to listen to what Mark wrote? He said a lot of things about Peter.

Anna: It was a little bit, Junia. I do miss Peter, but I know he's with the Lord.

Junia: I also wondered what you thought about the way Mark described Peter. I know that Mark was close to Peter, but he tells stories that make Peter seem like he didn't understand Jesus.

Anna: I know, but that's the way it was. I loved Peter, but he could be impulsive and thick-headed sometimes. But many people didn't really understand Jesus. Mary Magdalene was a faithful follower of Jesus after he healed her but she often said that she didn't quite know how to love him. The rest of the disciples didn't recognize who Jesus really was, and his family didn't either. His family thought Jesus was a public embarrassment.

Junia: That's right, but then Peter denied Jesus three times. It's not a very flattering picture.

Anna: No, it's not, and Peter carried a heavy burden of guilt over his denying Jesus. It meant so much to him that Jesus forgave him after God raised him from the dead.

Junia: Oh, when did that happen?

Anna: One time after Jesus rose from the dead, Jesus met the disciples up in Galilee while they were fishing. While they were eating on the lakeshore, Jesus asked Peter three times if Peter loved him. Each time Peter said "Yes," and then Jesus said, "Feed my lambs." It bothered Peter that Jesus had to ask him *three* times if he loved him, but afterward he saw that it was Jesus' way of forgiving him for denying him three times.

Junia: What a special story! Why didn't Mark include that in what he wrote about Jesus?

Anna: That's a good question. I was wondering the same thing.

Junia: Maybe we should ask him.

Anna:	It may be too late. He's boarding a ship tomorrow to go back to be with his family in Jerusalem.
Junia:	He is? Isn't that dangerous now with the war with Rome going on?
Anna:	I think so, but he thinks the situation here is just as dangerous.
Junia:	He may be right. Although now that Emperor Nero is dead, we may be safer.
Anna:	I don't know. I often feel afraid about what may happen to us.
Junia:	I know you're not alone. Many in our community are fearful — and uncertain about what to believe about Jesus.
Anna:	As I said, I share some of that fear, but not that uncertainty about Jesus. I feel fortunate that Peter and I experienced the risen Jesus and came to a fuller understanding of who he was and what he came to do. I think the story Mark wrote will help more people share that fuller understanding of Jesus.
Junia:	Do you think so? That brings me back to his ending. Mark seems to leave everything up in the air. He said that Mary Magdalene, the other Mary, and Salome responded to the empty tomb with fear and amazement. They were supposed to tell what they saw to the disciples but Mark wrote that they said nothing to anyone because they were afraid. Why end that way?
Anna:	Well, that was the truth. They were deeply upset. The whole experience seemed eerie and frightening. They weren't sure if they should be

afraid of grave robbers, or if something miraculous and out of this world had occurred. Eventually they did tell everyone.

Junia: True, but why not tell that?

Anna: Maybe because Mark wrote his story for us.

Junia: What do you mean?

Anna: Don't you feel like those women — sometimes fearful or uncertain or amazed at what happened with Jesus?

Junia: Yes, I do, and I know that others here share similar feelings.

Anna: Maybe Mark wants us to see ourselves in the women.

Junia: There's a certain comfort in doing that. If those women — and the other disciples and even his family — had doubts and fears, maybe there's hope for us. Maybe we can still be followers of Jesus.

Anna: Yes, Jesus included ordinary people among his disciples who weren't perfect in faith or courage or love. My Peter surely was an example of that.

Junia: If Mark wants us to compare ourselves with the women at the tomb, perhaps he leaves us with a question.

Anna: What question is that?

Junia: How do you respond to the empty tomb?

Anna: *(turning to the congregation)* Yes, how will *you* respond to the risen Jesus?

Johannine
Interviews

Week 1

Interview with Nicodemus

John 3:1-17

Narrator: Our news station has heard many reports about Jesus of Nazareth. To learn more about this Jesus we are interviewing several people who have witnessed him firsthand. Tonight we have sent Angela Evans to interview Nicodemus, a religious scholar and a member of the Sanhedrin, who met with Jesus so that he could understand him better. Angela...

Angela: This is Angela Evans, reporting for WALC-TV, outside a villa near the temple in Jerusalem. We are talking with Nicodemus, a leader among the Pharisees. Nicodemus, you have just returned from what you call a strange encounter. Whom did you meet with tonight?

Nicodemus: I met with Jesus of Nazareth, a teacher and miracle worker from Galilee, who is here in Jerusalem for the Passover festival.

Angela: Why did you meet with this Jesus?

Nicodemus: Angela, we have begun to hear reports about miracles he performed up in Galilee. They seem to have been signs indicating something special about him. Jesus also caused quite a disturbance a few days ago when he chased the merchants and money changers out of the temple area. His followers believe he has great devotion to pure worship of God. I wanted to find out for myself about this man.

Angela: Why did you tell me this was a "strange" encounter?

Nicodemus: This Jesus did not seem to be the kind of person I was expecting. I assumed he would be an ordinary teacher and miracle worker but his replies to my questions seemed like strange riddles to me.

Angela: Can you give us an example?

Nicodemus: When I asked if he was a teacher come from God, he replied that to see God's kingdom you must be born again. At least that's what I thought he said.

Angela: "That's what you *thought* he said." What did he really say?

Nicodemus: I'm not sure, but when I asked, "How in the world can someone enter his mother's womb and be born again?" he almost seemed to laugh at me and replied that to enter God's kingdom you have to be born of water and the wind.

Angela: Born of water and the wind? That is strange. What do you think he meant?

Nicodemus: By "born of water" he may have meant ordinary birth. Or, since some of his followers were also followers of John the Baptist, he may mean the religious washing of baptism. But the wind part, I don't understand.

Angela: Isn't it true that the word "wind" can also be used for the "Spirit" of God?

Nicodemus: Perhaps so. See how puzzling his speech is? He did say something about the contrast between earthly and heavenly things. Maybe he was saying that the kingdom of God has something to do with earthly things, perhaps even including our religious rituals, but also with heavenly things — things of the Spirit that can't always be predicted or controlled.

Angela: I wonder if there is another double meaning.

Nicodemus: What do you mean?

Angela: You said that Jesus told you that you must be "born again." But those words can also mean "born from above." Perhaps Jesus is saying that to be part of God's kingdom you must be born from above — that is, given a new spiritual birth through God's Spirit. And, as you said, this may mean a change that you can't predict or control. What changes do you think God's Spirit might bring to people who believe in this Jesus?

Nicodemus: That's a good question, but I don't know how to answer that question right now. But he said one more strange thing.

Angela: What was that?

Nicodemus: He said something about the Son of Man — he seemed to be talking about himself — must be "lifted up," just like Moses lifted up the serpent in the wilderness.

Angela: What did he mean by "lifted up"?

Nicodemus: That's another part of the puzzle. If we think of the story of Moses and the serpent in the wilderness, lifted up would mean being tied to a pole.

Angela: That sounds like being crucified to me.

Nicodemus: To me as well — a sad and depressing thought. But he made it sound like something more joyful or victorious, for it would lead to eternal life. Could crucifixion be a victory?

Angela: For our people crucifixion has usually meant cruel defeat and agonizing death.

Nicodemus: That's right, but Jesus gave no hint of talking about defeat. In fact he talked about how much God loves the world.

Angela: The world and not just God's own people?

Nicodemus: That's right — the world. Jesus said that God sent his Son — and Jesus seemed to be talking about himself — he said that God sent his Son, not to condemn the world, but to save it and to offer people eternal life.

Angela: Well, Nicodemus, what do you make of your encounter with Jesus?

Nicodemus: The experience is too fresh and puzzling for me, Angela, but Jesus does seem to have a message that God's Spirit will lead us in new directions and give us new birth in some way. I will want to watch and see how his being "lifted up" will save us.

Angela: Thank you, Nicodemus, for answering our questions about your strange encounter with this Jesus of Nazareth. Back to you in the studio at WALC.

Narrator: Thank you, Angela, for your interesting report.

Week 2

Interview with a Samaritan Woman

John 4:1-30

Narrator: Our news station has heard many reports about Jesus of Nazareth. To learn more about this Jesus we are interviewing several people who have witnessed him firsthand. Tonight we have sent Harold Evans to interview Leah, a woman from Samaria who had an interesting encounter with this Jesus earlier today. Harold...

Harold: This is Harold Evans, reporting for WALC-TV, outside the village of Sychar in Samaria. I'm talking with Leah, who caused quite a stir in Sychar earlier today when she reported an encounter with a wandering Jewish teacher by the name of Jesus. Leah, I understand you came hurrying into the village this afternoon, claiming that you had met the Messiah when you were getting water from Jacob's Well. Could you tell us what happened to make you say this?

Leah: Yes, Harold, but your question gets ahead of the story.

Harold: What do you mean?

Leah: I didn't think that he was anyone special at first. My ideas about him emerged only gradually.

Harold: What was your first impression?

Leah: Well, at first I was quite annoyed. I was coming at noon in the heat of the day, eager to fill my water jar from the well, and there was this Jewish man. I couldn't figure out why he was there, and I was afraid that I wouldn't be able to get my water.

Harold: Why not?

Leah: This situation was all wrong. Jews don't associate with us Samaritans, and men, whether Jew or Samaritan, aren't supposed to talk with women who aren't from their family.

Harold: Did he try to keep you away from the well?

Leah: Oh, no. He even spoke to me and asked for a drink of water.

Harold: Did you give him a drink?

Leah: Why, no. I asked him why he, a Jewish man, was asking me, a Samaritan woman, for a drink. Then he said that if I knew who he was, I'd ask him for some living water.

Harold: What is living water?

Leah: I'm not sure. I thought he meant running water, like in a river, instead of well water, but I didn't know how he could get any water since he didn't have a bucket. The truth is he offended me a bit, because I thought he was trying to say that he was better than our ancestor Jacob who first dug this well. Maybe, though, he meant something different, for he said that his water would keep people from ever getting thirsty. I think he said something about eternal life, but I was thinking about how great it would be if I always had enough water and didn't need to come to the well anymore.

Harold:	Is that when you began to think he was the Messiah?
Leah:	Not yet. Don't rush my story! Something else happened first.
Harold:	What was that?
Leah:	He asked me to get my husband. I tried to avoid his question, and then he said, "Right. You have had five husbands, and the man you are living with now is not your husband." I was shocked, for he seemed to know the whole truth about me.
Harold:	You seem to have been unfortunate in your relationships with men.
Leah:	That's one way of putting it. Twice widowed, three times divorced, I'm a little leery of relationships with men right now. But that's not the point.
Harold:	What is the point?
Leah:	That he knew the truth about me so exactly. I decided then that he must be a prophet.
Harold:	How did he react to that?
Leah:	He didn't really react, but we began to discuss the differences between Samaritan and Jewish religion. Then he said that true religion would go beyond the physical places where we both worship. God is a Spirit, and we should worship God in Spirit and in truth.
Harold:	What did he mean by that?
Leah:	I really don't know, but somehow it aroused in me a sense that this man was opening up for me a deeper understanding of God. That's when I

said something about the Messiah, and he said, "I am he."

Harold: He said that to you, a Samaritan woman?

Leah: That is quite amazing, isn't it? I understand that this is the first time he said who he is so publicly.

Harold: Really? I wonder what this says about this Jesus if he chose to reveal his special identity first to you.

Leah: I agree that is an important question. He seemed to mean that worshiping God goes beyond the divisions we have often built between us.

Harold: Now that this day is almost over, what does it mean for you?

Leah: I'm sure I'll be thinking it over for a while. I've learned two things today: First, I'm convinced that this Jesus is special and he is here to help us have a deeper relationship with God. Also he has shown me that God knows and cares about each one of us, whether we're Jewish or Samaritan, woman or man.

Harold: Would you like to get some of his water?

Leah: His water?

Harold: Yes, the living water he talked about.

Leah: Yes, I would. Do you think this living water has something to do with worshiping God in spirit and in truth?

Harold: Perhaps — and maybe bringing the eternal life you said he mentioned.

Leah: This has been a special day. My thirst has been satisfied in several ways! But my appetite has also been whetted for more of this living water from Jesus.

Harold: Thank you, Leah, for answering our questions about your encounter with this Jesus at Jacob's Well. Back to you in the studio at WALC.

Narrator: Thank you, Harold, for an illuminating report.

The Adulterous Woman — An Interview

John 7:53—8:11

Narrator: Our news station has heard many reports about Jesus of Nazareth. Today we learned about a confrontation involving this Jesus inside the temple grounds in Jerusalem. We have sent Harold Evans to interview a woman who witnessed this scene today. Harold...

Harold: This is Harold Evans of WALC-TV, coming to you live from Jerusalem, just outside the temple grounds. We had quite a stir this morning inside the temple in the Court of the Gentiles, where Jesus of Nazareth, a traveling teacher and miracle worker from Galilee, was teaching a crowd of people. Some scribes and Pharisees came rushing up to Jesus, dragging with them a woman they claimed had been caught in the act of adultery. They asked Jesus what he thought should be done. They seemed to have every intention of stoning her to death, as provided for in the Law of Moses. After confronting Jesus with this situation, however, they let the woman go and surprisingly they all walked away. We have been told that the woman's name is Mary, but she declined our request to talk with her. I'm talking with Joanna, who says she is her cousin and knows her well. Joanna, what happened this morning?

Joanna: This is not easy for me to talk about, Harold. Today has been a very upsetting day.

Harold: I can understand that. Can you tell us how your cousin Mary happened to be caught by some scribes and Pharisees and brought to Jesus?

Joanna: First of all, I am upset with my cousin. I've always thought she was a good and pious person. I'm so disappointed with her.

Harold: Was she really caught in an adulterous act?

Joanna: Yes, she was found in bed with her neighbor. Her husband was visiting relatives in Jericho. This is so out of character for Mary.

Harold: So you are mostly upset with your cousin?

Joanna: Oh, no, that isn't the half of it. I'm upset with those Pharisees.

Harold: Why is that?

Joanna: Well, first because they brought only Mary to Jesus. What about that man? The Law of Moses says that both adulterer and adulteress should be put to death. This is just another example of women being treated unfairly. And besides I don't think they really cared about Mary or that man; I think they were just looking for some excuse to challenge Jesus. I'm upset because I think they used my cousin like some piece of meat so that they could see what Jesus would say about the Law of Moses. They didn't care about how embarrassing this would be for her and her family.

Harold: Do you feel embarrassed by what happened today?

Joanna: Yes, wouldn't you?

Harold: I suppose. But tell us now what happened when they brought your cousin to Jesus. Were you there?

Joanna: Yes, I saw the whole sorry event, although it wasn't so sorry in the end.

Harold: What do you mean?

Joanna: Well, these scribes brought Mary to Jesus and asked him what should be done with her. This Jesus sure can be strange!

Harold: Why do you say that?

Joanna: Because at first he said nothing and was writing in the dirt.

Harold: Really? What was he writing?

Joanna: I don't know. I couldn't see. Some people thought he was listing the sins of her accusers. Finally he stood up and said, "Let the person without sin cast the first stone."

Harold: So he agreed with the punishment in the Law of Moses then?

Joanna: I guess you could say that, but something surprising happened next.

Harold: What was that?

Joanna: Miraculously no one picked up a stone and threw it at her. Somehow Jesus' response made this entire hypocritical group be honest and admit that they weren't perfect either. They all walked away silently.

Harold: What happened next?

Joanna: Jesus went back to writing in the dirt. After everyone else went away, he stood up, looked Mary right in the eye, and asked, "Woman, did no one condemn you?" She said, "No, sir." Then he said an amazing thing, "Neither do I condemn you. Go, and sin no more."

Harold: How did your cousin react to this?

Joanna: First of all, she does feel embarrassed that she disgraced herself and her family by what she did, and she is angry with how these people treated her so roughly and unfairly. But she feels a strange kind of joy because of what this Jesus said and did.

Harold: That's surprising. Why would she feel joy after this upsetting incident? Is she happy that she was spared being killed by stoning?

Joanna: Yes, that's part of it, of course, but it is more than that. She told me that she felt that Jesus treated her in a special way. She felt as if he recognized her as a real person. He didn't treat her as some *thing* to make a point. He looked her in the eye and made her feel that he really cared for her, and then he forgave her.

Harold: So her joy came from being forgiven?

Joanna: Yes, but she recognizes that there's still more. She heard what he said about not sinning any more. She knows that will be difficult, maybe impossible, but Jesus treating her with respect and compassion has made her want to try because she believes again that God loves her.

Harold: It sounds like Jesus gave your cousin a double message.

Joanna: What do you mean?

Harold: On the one hand, he told her that he didn't condemn her. On the other, he told her not to sin any more. Doesn't that sound contradictory?

Joanna: That's not how Mary and I understood Jesus. We felt that Jesus offered her forgiveness first. As a response to that forgiveness he encouraged her to turn back to following God's will for us. That's not a double message; that's two sides of the same coin. Forgiveness and response go together.

Harold: So knowing God's forgiveness leads us to live like God wants us to live?

Joanna: That's what we think.

Harold: Well, your cousin Mary did have a full day! Thank you for sharing your story with us. Back to you in the studio of WALC.

Narrator: Thank you, Harold, for your thought-provoking report on a surprising encounter with Jesus of Nazareth.

An Interview with Jairus, the Man Born Blind

John 9:1-38

Narrator: Our news station has heard many reports about Jesus of Nazareth. To learn more about this Jesus we are interviewing several people who have witnessed him firsthand. Tonight we have sent Angela Evans to interview Jairus, a blind man who apparently experienced one of the miracles reportedly performed by Jesus. Angela...

Angela: This is Angela Evans, reporting for WALC-TV, talking with Jairus by the Pool of Siloam, where he experienced a life-changing event earlier today. Jairus, can you tell our audience what happened to you today?

Jairus: Yes, Angela, I did have a life-changing experience today. I started out this morning as a blind man, as I have been my whole life, but now I can see.

Angela: That's amazing! How did this happen?

Jairus: This Jesus, a teacher and healer from Galilee, and his disciples came past the place where I usually sit to beg and ask for alms. I heard them talking about me.

Angela: What were they saying about you?

Jairus:	His disciples asked him who sinned, my parents or me, to make me blind from birth. That kind of talk makes me so angry. I've heard it so often. Doesn't anyone know the book of Job? God made it very clear to Job's friends that they were wrong to accuse Job of doing something wrong. I was ready to set them all straight, but then I was surprised by the teacher's response.
Angela:	What surprised you?
Jairus:	Well, this Jesus totally disagreed with his disciples. He said what I've always believed — and my blindness was not a punishment for sin, neither my parents' nor mine. Then he added that the purpose of my blindness was to reveal the work of God.
Angela:	What did he mean by that?
Jairus:	I don't know, but before I had time to muster up the courage to ask him what he meant, he rubbed mud on my eyes and told me to wash it off here in the Pool of Siloam. I did and now I can see!
Angela:	That must have been some special kind of mud!
Jairus:	That's what I thought at first, but then I realized it wasn't the mud that was special. Like he said, this blindness of mine was intended to reveal the work of God. It was God who caused this miracle, not the mud.
Angela:	However this miracle happened, you must be very happy to be able to see.

Jairus:	Yes, I am happy, but I do feel overwhelmed by all this visual stimuli that I've never had before. It's going to take me a while to get used to seeing everything that I've only touched or heard before. But not everyone shares my happiness.
Angela:	Who wouldn't be happy for you?
Jairus:	Some of the Pharisees.
Angela:	Why didn't they share your joy?
Jairus:	They seemed upset by what happened to me. I gather that they are like Jesus' disciples and think my blindness was a punishment for sin. Plus they said that this Jesus is a sinner.
Angela:	Why would they think that someone who performed a miracle like this would be a sinner?
Jairus:	A good question, but he did break our sabbath laws by doing work — making this mud and healing me while it was still the sabbath.
Angela:	Doing good by curing someone's blindness violates the sabbath?
Jairus:	Well, I don't think so — and this Jesus apparently doesn't think so — but our rabbis do argue about whether or not the command to rest on the sabbath prohibits works of healing.
Angela:	So they see this Jesus as a sinner. What do you think?
Jairus:	I don't see him as a sinner! At first, I saw him as a prophet, but then the wonder of what he did overwhelmed me. I came to see him as the Son of Man, that special person sent from God. When he talked with me after I could see, all I could do was worship him. Yes, my blindness

	revealed the work of God, and this Jesus was the one doing the work of God.
Angela:	So you really are saying that you have come to see many different things today.
Jairus:	Yes, for the first time I've seen people, including my parents, and birds and trees and donkeys and flowers....
Angela:	Yes, yes, but I mean more than that. Not only do you see all those things, but where those Pharisees see a sinner you have seen God at work.
Jairus:	Oh, yes, I have gained different levels of vision. This is another way that I feel overwhelmed.
Angela:	What do you mean?
Jairus:	Well, now that I have recognized God at work in Jesus, what do I do about it? I once was blind but now I see.
Angela:	It seems that you have answered your question in one way — you are talking about Jesus and what he did for you.
Jairus:	That's right. I can't help but share my story of receiving my sight back because of what Jesus did.
Angela:	It sounds, though, as if this experience will mean even more for you.
Jairus:	That's for sure. I'm wondering if after what happened today, my life can stay the same. But how shall it change?
Angela:	A good question! We'll have to come back another time to see how you answer it. Now back to you in the studio at WALC-TV.

Narrator: Thank you, Angela, for your enlightening report on this apparent miracle by Jesus of Nazareth.

An Interview
with Mary of Bethany

John 11:1-44

Narrator: Our news station has heard many reports about Jesus of Nazareth. To learn more about this Jesus we are interviewing several people who have witnessed him firsthand. Tonight we have sent Harold Evans to interview Mary from Bethany, whose brother Lazarus was allegedly brought back to life by Jesus. Harold...

Harold: This is Harold Evans, reporting for WALC-TV, outside the home of Lazarus in Bethany. I had hoped to interview Lazarus himself, but he is secluded with the rest of his family here in his home. I'm talking instead with his sister Mary. Mary, can you tell us what happened today?

Mary: Yes, Harold, this has been quite a momentous day for us. This morning we were grieving the death of our brother, Lazarus, four days ago. Tonight we are sharing our evening meal with him.

Harold: You must be very happy.

Mary: You would think so, wouldn't you? Of course, we're happy that Lazarus is alive again, but this whole experience has been extremely

	overwhelming. We feel numb and not quite sure how to react.
Harold:	Ewww, what's that smell?
Mary:	Oh, I'm sorry! That's from Lazarus' grave clothes. He was in the tomb four days after all. Let's move away from where we left them.
Harold:	That's better. Now can you tell us what happened? I understand that Jesus of Nazareth was here today.
Mary:	Yes, Jesus was here today. My brother, Lazarus, is a beloved follower of his. When Lazarus took ill a week ago, we sent word to Jesus across the Jordan where he was spending time with his other disciples. We thought Jesus would come quickly and heal our brother.
Harold:	He didn't come right away?
Mary:	No, he didn't arrive until today. My sister, Martha, and I both told him that we thought Lazarus would have lived if he had come sooner. Some of his other disciples told us that Jesus told them that he delayed coming to show the glory of God. I'm beginning to see why he said that, but I didn't understand that this morning.
Harold:	What did he say when you said Lazarus would have lived if he had come sooner?
Mary:	He didn't say anything to me, but he told my sister that he is the resurrection and the life. We believe that because we have seen how he has the power to heal people. From what Martha told me, though, Jesus seemed to mean more than his power to heal. He said

	something about people who believe in him living, even though they die, and people who live never dying. We believe the righteous shall rise on the last day, but Jesus didn't seem to like that when Martha said it.
Harold:	How did Jesus react when you went to the tomb?
Mary:	Even though we are friends, Jesus can be confusing to me. He did weep, and I thought he was grieving with us. But he also seemed upset — angry even.
Harold:	Why would he be angry or upset?
Mary:	That's a good question. I think it has something to do with what his other disciples told us. Jesus loves Lazarus but he didn't come here just to do what we wanted and give us another healing miracle. No, he came here to show how his raising Lazarus is a sign of the glory of God. I've come to see him as God's own Son, but I think our family has been accustomed to seeing him as an important teacher or miracle worker but not anything more.
Harold:	So this day has led you to develop a new understanding of Jesus?
Mary:	Yes, but it hasn't worked that way for everyone.
Harold:	What do you mean?
Mary:	Well, many of our friends from Jerusalem have come to believe in Jesus as revealing God's glory because of what happened today, but I have heard rumors that some others are upset with him. They fear that if he does more

signs like this, the Romans may punish us somehow.

Harold: No wonder you don't feel totally happy today. That thought seems frightening to me.

Mary: Yes, it is, and I fear that Jesus may face death because of this opposition.

Harold: That would be ironic: his giving life to Lazarus might bring him death.

Mary: Yes, I'm trying to think of some way that I can express my devotion to Jesus, show him what I have come to see in him, and maybe somehow prepare him for what he might be facing.

Harold: What might you do?

Mary: We have invited Jesus to have dinner with us in a few days. I might want to buy some special perfume to wash his feet instead of plain water.

Harold: Why would you do that?

Mary: I think that would symbolize how much I honor and value him. But there's something else that I wonder about.

Harold: What's that?

Mary: Jesus says he is the resurrection and the life. Does that mean even his own death will not defeat him? And what would that mean for us?

Harold: Those are deep questions. We will be waiting to see if you find answers to those questions any time soon. Now back to you in the studio at WALC-TV.

Narrator: Thank you, Harold, for your thorough report on another surprising event involving Jesus of Nazareth.

Affirming Our Baptismal Promises

Week 1

To Live Among God's Faithful People

Hebrews 10:19-25

Narrator: Two people are talking during a church's coffee hour following a service welcoming Nova and other new members and using an Affirmation of Baptism service.

Angela: Hi, Nova! I'm glad to see that you're a member now.

Nova: Oh, hi, Angela. I think I'm glad too.

Angela: What do you mean, "think"? Aren't you sure?

Nova: I was glad until Pastor made us make that promise up there.

Angela: What promise was that?

Nova: You know — that promise where he asked, "You have made public profession of your faith. Do you intend to continue in the covenant God made with you in Holy Baptism — to live among God's faithful people..." and all the rest.

Angela: Wow! I'm impressed that you remembered all those words.

Nova: Well, I was the one up there making that promise. I noticed the words.

Angela: What bothered you about making that promise?

Nova: Well, I think it's a pretty heavy-duty promise. I'm not sure I'm up to keeping it.

Angela: I wouldn't worry about it too much. Everybody says the same words.

Nova: Are you telling me that I shouldn't take it seriously?

Angela: No, I don't mean that. I guess you're right — you should take it seriously. But why do you think it's such a difficult promise?

Nova: Well, think about the first line, "to live among God's faithful people." It sounds like we're supposed to join a religious commune.

Angela: Oh, Nova, it doesn't mean that! Do we look like a religious commune?

Nova: No, you don't, or I wouldn't have joined here. I guess it probably doesn't mean that, but does it mean that we're supposed to come to church every Sunday?

Angela: That wouldn't be a bad idea.

Nova: But we can't! I have to be out of town on business some weekends, and we go to visit our parents out of state too.

Angela: You could find another church to go to wherever you are on a weekend.

Nova: I suppose you're right, but it's not always easy when you have some business or family commitments.

Angela: I know, so I guess those are legitimate reasons. I think the promise means that you'll worship as regularly as you're able.

Nova: Does the congregation have some quota, some number of times you have to worship during the year or you're out?

Angela: You know, I think you're looking at this the wrong way. It's not so much that you've "got to" worship but that you "get to" worship.

Nova: What do you mean?

Angela: When we affirm our baptism, we remind ourselves that God has chosen us and that God has made us part of God's family. Our worshiping and the other things we do are ways that we express our gratefulness for what God has done for us.

Nova: So coming to worship is an expression of gratitude?

Angela: Right. So it's not a matter of keeping a record of perfect church attendance and getting gold stars next to your name on some master list like we used to do for Sunday school attendance.

Nova: Used to do? Don't you do that any more? I always liked seeing those gold stars next to my name when I was in Sunday school.

Angela: Actually I'm not sure what we do in Sunday school since I don't have kids in Sunday school, but I know we don't do it for church attendance.

Nova: So no special award for perfect church attendance?

Angela: No, there isn't — sorry if that disappoints you! Coming to worship is more a matter of finding as many opportunities to praise God as we can

	because we are grateful for God's blessings. But that's not all.
Nova:	What else is there? Is there some scorekeeping after all?
Angela:	No! Coming to church isn't only about thanking God. It's also about being together with other Christians.
Nova:	Really? When I grew up, we just went to church to get the service over, and then we went home as soon as we could. Socializing with other church members wasn't important for us.
Angela:	That surprises me! Here our fellowship with other members is very important to us.
Nova:	So I've noticed — and that is something that I do appreciate about this church.
Angela:	And our fellowship is important to us because that's one way "to live among God's faithful people."
Nova:	So faith is not just me and God; it's also me and other believers?
Angela:	Right. And it's important to come to church regularly to strengthen our fellowship — to develop relationships so that we can care for each other — so that we can share our faith and Christian love with each other.
Nova:	That doesn't sound so burdensome. These are the kind of relationships we want now in our church. Maybe that part of the promise isn't so bad. But the other parts —
Angela:	What do you mean?

Nova: I'll ask you about them some other time. Right now I want to get some coffee and cookies before they're all gone. Are you sure no one keeps score of how often we attend church?

Angela: Yes, I'm sure — and save me some cookies too!

Week 2

To Hear the Word of God and Share in the Lord's Supper

Romans 10:10-18

Narrator: Nova and Angela resume their conversation from last week's coffee hour.

Angela: Hi, Nova, how was your week?

Nova: Oh, hi, Angela! Aside from spinning out on the Tri-State Toll Road[1] last Friday and my computer crashing at work, not too bad.

Angela: That doesn't sound good. I'm glad my week was dull in comparison.

Nova: Yes, sometimes dull is good. But my car and I didn't get hurt, and my computer is up and running again.

Angela: That's good. Do you still have questions from last week? It sounded like you had more to say about your Affirmation of Baptism promises when we ran out of time.

Nova: Well, I do have more concerns. You said last week that there's no quota for how often we have to worship.

Angela: Remember that I said that it's not that we've **got** to worship but that we **get** to worship.

Nova: Okay, okay, worship is a grateful response to God's love. But I still wonder if there's a hidden quota someplace.

Angela: Why do you think that?

Nova: Well, remember the next part of the promise: "Do you promise to hear the word of God and share in the Lord's Supper"? Doesn't that refer to worship?

Angela: I guess it does, but there's still no hidden quota.

Nova: Are you sure?

Angela: Yes! Do you like to eat?

Nova: That's a dumb question. Of course I do! Don't you remember that I first came to our church for the Oktoberfest?[2] And my favorite TV show is "Check, Please!"[3]

Angela: Well, does anyone tell you that you have to come to dinner?

Nova: No — not unless I get so caught up with working on the computer that I forget what time it is. But no, eating is something I do willingly. So what?

Angela: Well, coming to church to hear God's word and to receive Communion is like religious eating — it feeds our faith.

Nova: Now that you mention it, church does seem like an Italian restaurant.

Angela: Why in the world would you say that? We're not all Italian here so how would we be like an Italian restaurant?

Nova: Now be careful! I'm not talking about our ethnic heritage. Haven't we gotten rid of all those ethnic divisions among the churches?

Angela: I guess so, but I still don't understand what you mean.

Nova: Well, worship is like the courses you have in some Italian restaurants. The gathering part is like the antipasto, the word portion is like the pasta course, the meal section is the entrée, and the sending is like the dessert course.

Angela: That is a clever comparison. You're right — all four parts of worship are about feeding our faith. Of course, that's more obvious with Communion since it still includes the bread and wine that once was part of a full meal early Christians shared. Yes, we have both reading and preaching and Communion because we think it's important for our faith to be fed during our Sunday worship.

Nova: I appreciate that. I know some people think that Communion can lose its importance if you receive it too often, but I think you can never receive the presence of Christ in your life too often. Besides, I value the sense of being together with other Christians Sunday by Sunday around the altar.

Angela: So if you agree that worship is like eating for the soul, does your promise seem less burdensome?

Nova: Yes, I'll go along with that.

Angela: I think I should add something though.

Nova: Uh-oh, here comes the quota!

Angela: Don't be so paranoid! What I want to add is that hearing the word of God isn't limited to worship. You can hear the word of God on the radio or even online. You can hear the word of God in our various study groups. You can hear it in your own personal reading.

Nova: I'm going to have to do that because I really would like to learn more about the Bible's message. Maybe I could even learn enough so that I could lead a Bible study.

Angela: That sounds like a good idea.

Nova: Maybe — but my feet are too ugly.

Angela: You sure are saying some strange things today. What in the world do your feet have to do with it?

Nova: Don't you know the Bible reading that says "How beautiful are the feet of those who bring good news"? I don't think I'm eligible to bring good news because my feet are ugly. Do you want to see them?

Angela: No, I don't! You do know that's a metaphor, right? Helping people grow in their faith is a beautiful thing.

Nova: Yes, I suppose I do know that. I guess my ugly feet don't give me an excuse not to share my faith. But that's something for another day.

Angela: So still another sequel? Let's get some coffee before it's too late.

---

1. A major highway in the Chicago metropolitan area. Substitute the name of an appropriate highway for your area.

2. Ascension Lutheran Church had an Oktoberfest dinner for fellowship and fund-raising. Substitute a similar event from your congregation's life.

3. A local PBS show in the Chicago area about the participants' favorite restaurants. Perhaps you could substitute *Diners, Drive-ins and Dives*, *Barefoot Contessa*, or another chef show from the Food Network.

To Proclaim the Good News of God in Christ Through Word and Deed

Matthew 5:13-16; Luke 8:19-21

Narrator: Nova and Angela have been talking about the promises Nova made as part of the Affirmation of Baptism service that was used on the day he was welcomed as a new member. The last time they talked Nova made it sound as if he had still more questions. Nova and Angela run into each other in the grocery store.

Angela: Oh, hi, Nova! I didn't expect to see you here.

Nova: Hi, Angela! Oh, yeah, I shop here a lot. Remember how I said that I love food? Well, I like to cook too, so I often do the grocery shopping. Seeing you, Angela, reminds me of another concern I have.

Angela: What's that?

Nova: Those promises I made seem to commit me to sharing my faith.

Angela: What makes you say that?

Nova: One of the things we had to promise was "to proclaim the good news of God in Christ through word and deed." I don't know — I don't mind being a church member but that sounds like I'm supposed to be a preacher.

Angela: I hope that's not what it means. I'd rather be trapped in a cage full of snakes than speak in front of a bunch of people!

Nova: So is that why you don't read in church?

Angela: Right. Let me organize a church potluck but don't make me say something in church!

Nova: Well, if that promise doesn't mean preaching, what does it mean?

Angela: I think I heard our pastor quote Saint Francis once, "Always preach the gospel; if necessary use words."

Nova: How does that go? "Always preach the gospel; if necessary use words"?

Angela: That's right. That reassured me that there may be many ways to share our faith; some are by word, some are by deed.

Nova: I'm relieved I wasn't promising to become a preacher. I was especially worried that I might have to stand on some street corner, handing out tracts and asking people if they had found Jesus.

Angela: No, that's not our style, although we might do similar things.

Nova: Like what?

Angela: Well, I handed out refrigerator magnets with our picture and contact information on it while some of us marched in the village Fourth of July parade. And I know that some churches go door to door asking people if they have a church home.

Nova: If I don't have to be a preacher in church or on a street corner, what might I be expected to do?

Angela: That's difficult to answer, because the answer depends on you and what opportunities you have. You could begin right here and now.

Nova: Share my faith in a grocery store? Am I supposed to preach to the tomatoes and lettuce?

Angela: No! But see that elderly woman over there trying to get a box off the top shelf? You're tall enough — maybe you could help her.

Nova: Yes, I could do that.

Angela: Here's a more difficult one. See that mother with the three children who seem out of control? I think she's about to lose it.

Nova: What can I do? Strange men aren't usually welcome to help with children they don't know these days.

Angela: You're right. But see that box she dropped? You could pick it up and give it to her. Maybe doing that would interrupt her enough to keep her from lashing out in anger at her crying child.

Nova: I know another possibility. One of the clerks is new to the job, and she makes mistakes in giving out change. I could give it back when she gives me too much change.

Angela: Right. So those are opportunities to proclaim the good news in deed. What about in word?

Nova: I was hoping I could avoid doing that.

Angela: No such luck! There may be times when it is necessary — or times when you have an opportunity too good to pass up.

Nova: Like what?

Angela: You might overhear someone in the checkout line mention that they've just moved to town. You could welcome them to town and say that if they're looking for a church you can recommend one.

Nova: Not a bad idea but that might be a stretch for someone as shy as me.

Angela: Well, suppose one of those people you helped ask you why you did it. What would you say?

Nova: I would probably say, "It was nothing" or mumble something inaudible.

Angela: Why not say "because I'm a Christian" or "because God loves me and wants me to love others"?

Nova: That's possible, I guess.

Angela: Remember, the Bible says "always be ready to give an account of the hope that's within you." You don't have to preach on a street corner, but you can be ready to share your faith when someone asks you about it.

Nova: Like Jesus said, "Let your light shine before others."

Angela: Right. And don't cover it with a basket.

Nova: I must say that I never thought of a grocery store as such an arena for "proclaiming good news."

Angela: Maybe it won't be a grocery store for you, but you can never tell when an opportunity to share your faith will present itself.

Nova: This has been a great conversation, but I'd better take the opportunity to check out soon or my ice cream is going to melt.

Angela: You're right. Dripping ice cream on the floor is probably not a good way to share faith! See you in church Sunday!

Nova: I look forward to it because I still have other questions.

To Serve All People, Following the Example of Jesus

Luke 22:24-27

Narrator: Nova and Angela meet again during their church's coffee hour after talking in the grocery store the past week.

Nova: I'm glad you're here this morning, Angela. I've been waiting to ask you those questions I said I had for you.

Angela: Well, here I am! What's the first question?

Nova: Can I wash your feet?

Angela: Are you kidding? I don't let anyone wash my feet! Do you know how many times I've told Pastor "No!" when he's asked me to be part of the foot washing on Maundy Thursday?

Nova: If I don't live up to the promises I made in my Affirmation of Baptism service, it will be all your fault.

Angela: Whoa! Don't make me responsible for your spiritual failings! What exactly are you talking about?

Nova: Well, I promised "to serve all people, following the example of Jesus," and since Jesus washed the feet of his disciples, I assumed that I should wash people's feet too.

Angela: Don't take your promise so literally. If you understand your promise that way, then you would get yourself crucified too.

Nova: I was hoping that washing feet might save me from being crucified.

Angela: Don't count on it. It didn't work that way for Jesus.

Nova: Okay. But if following the example of Jesus doesn't mean washing feet, what does it mean?

Angela: What do you think "washing feet" might symbolize?

Nova: Doing something that is humbling but provides a helpful service.

Angela: Right. Remember what Jesus said the night he did the foot washing: "I am among you as one who serves." We promise to serve other people in the same spirit Jesus showed, even if we don't do exactly the same things.

Nova: Okay, I won't go around trying to wash feet. But what should I do?

Angela: Love people by caring for their needs even if it means humbling yourself.

Nova: That's a nice mouthful, but what *exactly* should I do?

Angela: There's no single answer, Nova. It depends on what your talents are and what opportunities you have. Didn't you tell me that you love to cook?

Nova: Yes, I do. I've been reading a cookbook about soup recipes from monasteries.

Angela: Interesting. Then one thing you can do is prepare a stew for our midweek soup suppers.

Nova: I've been thinking about that. Yes, I could do that. But somehow cooking soup for church members doesn't seem totally like Jesus' humble service.

Angela: Jesus did wash his *disciples'* feet. But if you want to help people beyond our congregation, you could cook for the homeless people in the B.E.D.S. shelter.[1]

Nova: That's a good idea. And I do like how we try to help others through our monthly mission projects or by announcing other programs for helping people.

Angela: Yes, following Jesus' example can take many forms. I also think that ways for serving like Jesus can be found in all of our day-to-day relationships.

Nova: What do you mean?

Angela: Well, you work, don't you?

Nova: Yes. So what?

Angela: Don't you supervise a number of people?

Nova: Yes, about ten or so.

Angela: Then you can follow Jesus' example by treating them fairly and respectfully. And the same follows for your family.

Nova: Does that mean I have to be nice to my bossy sister who has irritated me all my life?

Angela: In short, yes. In fairness to you, though, being "nice" to someone doesn't mean ignoring how they annoy you, but it does mean treating the

Nova: person with love and respect and trying to find ways to work through what irritates you.

Nova: I see that there are many ways to follow Jesus' example, but what does it mean to "serve *all* people"? How impossible it is to serve *all* people! This is another reason why I think the promise I made is so unrealistic.

Angela: I admit that the promise sounds unrealistic. I think it means that there are no artificial boundaries around God's love. It doesn't mean that we are literally to serve every last person. I think it does mean that there is no particular person who is beyond the scope of our call to serve. Not only did Jesus serve by doing a humble job like washing feet, but he also served by associating with tax collectors and sinners.

Nova: Does that mean I have to serve Cubs[2] fans if I have the chance?

Angela: I'm afraid so, but it also means being ready to serve all kinds of people who are different from us — people who are rich or poor, young or old, black or white, Spanish-speaking or Anglo, friends or enemies. The list goes on.

Nova: This just shows that I'm right. There's no way I can keep my promise!

Angela: In a way you're right. There's no way we can follow Jesus' example perfectly. But I think the promise means we'll lead our lives in Jesus' spirit, always ready to serve others the way Jesus did in whatever situation we find ourselves.

Nova: Thank you, Angela, for helping me to see that my promise was not impossible exactly — only very challenging. But I think the last part of the promise is the worst.

Angela: Let's not talk about that now. You've got me tired out from thinking so hard. Can it keep till next week?

Nova: Okay, as long as you promise not to run away when I come up to you with my last question!

---

1. This acronym, which stands for "Building Ecumenical Discipleship through Sheltering," was the name for a local shelter program for homeless people. Substitute the name of a local homeless shelter or a similar program that provides meals.

2. Nova is a Chicago White Sox fan. Substitute an appropriate sports team name that might reflect a similar rivalry.

To Strive for Justice and Peace in All the Earth

Micah 6:6-8

Narrator: Nova meets Angela as he is entering their local food pantry carrying a box filled with cans of soup.

Angela: Oh, hi, Nova! I didn't expect to see you here. What are you doing?

Nova: I'm bringing a box of soup cans to our food pantry. What brings you here, Angela?

Angela: Oh, I was just dropping off some food too. You said last week that you had something else you wanted to ask me about, because the last part of the Affirmation of Baptism promise was the worst. What did you want to ask me?

Nova: Well, this may take a while — let me set this box down. What concerns me is that the last part of the promise is "to strive for justice and peace in all the earth." That really seems unrealistic, more unrealistic than the other parts of the promise. I mean, the United Nations can't establish "justice and peace in all the earth." How in the world can I be expected to do that?

Angela: Nova, I'm glad you're taking your promise seriously. But notice that you promised to *strive* for justice and peace in all the earth; you didn't promise to *accomplish* them.

Nova: That's a good point, Angela, and it does make the promise less daunting. But even merely *striving* for justice and peace in all the earth seems unrealistic.

Angela: I suppose it does seem that way, but in a way that promise has less to do with us and more to do with who our God is.

Nova: What do you mean? I thought it was *I* who made the promise.

Angela: Oh, you did, but the promise recognizes that we affirm our faith in a God who cares about justice and peace. Probably the most often mentioned concern in the Bible is justice — justice for the poor, for widows, orphans, and strangers.

Nova: So I am promising to care about justice and peace since my God cares about justice and peace.

Angela: Right.

Nova: But in *all* the earth?

Angela: Sure — because our God is a God who cares for everyone. God's concern for justice and peace isn't limited to just us.

Nova: Oh, that's cute. We might want a God who cares for "just us," but our God cares about "justice for all."

Angela: Right! And also remember that our God doesn't abandon us to work on this alone. God works with us to encourage and support us.

Nova: Good, because I'm going to need God's help!

Angela: So do we all, but I don't want you to think that your promise is totally unrealistic. It's important for us to keep in mind that our God cares about justice and peace and to think about ways we can work for them.

Nova: But what in the world can I do? I'm just one person.

Angela: Maybe not much, but the cumulative effect of small acts of individuals can lead to powerful consequences. Did you notice my "STOP" pin?

Nova: I did, but I wasn't sure I should mention it. It doesn't seem to be your style of jewelry.

Angela: Well, it's not jewelry.

Nova: What is it then?

Angela: This is the pin I got for being one of the top fund-raisers for our community CROP Walk last year. The "STOP" button is the CROP Walk's symbol for saying that they want to "stop hunger."

Nova: What in the world is a "CROP Walk"?

Angela: It's an annual fund-raising event to raise money for programs to alleviate hunger both overseas and locally too.

Nova: Why a "CROP" Walk? Do you collect food from local farmers' crops?

Angela: No! This program began after World War II, and farmers in our country did work to send food to people recovering from that war. The acronym meant "Christian Rural Overseas Project." It doesn't mean that any more, but we've kept the acronym because it became so familiar.

Nova: So one way to strive for justice and peace is do something to help people who are hungry?

Angela: That's right.

Nova: Aren't I doing that by bringing soup to the food pantry?

Angela: What you're doing is important, but it's not eradicating hunger. Concern for justice means not only feeding people, but also trying to change situations that contribute to people being hungry.

Nova: How can I do that?

Angela: Well, later this year we're going to have our annual offering of letters for Bread for the World. Bread for the World encourages us to write letters to our representatives in Washington to ask them to support government action on behalf of hungry people. This is one way to "strive for justice."

Nova: I don't know — I don't like to get involved in politics.

Angela: I guess it is getting involved in politics, but justice and peace are political issues. But it's not like partisan politics — it's telling the people who represent us that as Christians we care about issues of justice and encouraging them to find ways to create a more just society.

Nova: That's one suggestion. What if I'm more interested in something else?

Angela: Like what?

Nova: I'm not sure right now, but I do have a lot of different interests.

Angela: The issues of justice and peace that we can work on are almost endless — homelessness, health care, immigration, the environment, peace in the Middle East. If there is any justice or peace issue you'd like to work on, I'm sure we can find some way for you to help.

Nova: Now that we've talked about this, I can see that there are all kinds of interesting possibilities. Somehow my promise seems less unrealistic and more like encouragement to work on God's will for our world. If I come up with some project to work on, will you help me?

Angela: Uh-oh, I think I've gotten myself into something! Well, let me know what it is, and I'll be glad to see about helping. Now I'd better be on my way before I'm towed for parking too long in that space over there!